WARM-UPS and EXER[CISES]

for the Blues/Rock Guitarist

By Buzz Feiten

Recording Credits
Guitar: Buzz Feiten
Drums: Jason Smith
B-3: J.T. Thomas
Bass: Jorgen Carlson

Cover artwork by Levin Pfeufer
Photographs Courtesy of Aleksandra Sever (www.aleksandrasever.com)

Cherry Lane Music Company
Educational Director/Project Supervisor: Susan Poliniak
Director of Publications: Mark Phillips
Publications Coordinator: Rebecca Skidmore

ISBN 978-1-60378-178-7

 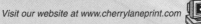

CONTENTS

INTRODUCTION

The Basics of Practice

I have been very fortunate. Growing up, I had parents who were both musicians, and they understood the importance of good teachers. I started studying piano when I was seven years old and, from the beginning, I learned some basics about practicing that have served me very well for over 40 years. In fact, I never actually studied guitar. When I realized that guitar was my passion, I just applied the general practice techniques that I had learned studying piano and taught myself how to play the guitar. These techniques apply to learning *any* musical instrument—not just guitar. These basics are my "Bible," and they consist of the following.

1. Mind your body position.

    a. Sit up straight.
        The act of straightening up tends to make you more focused.

    b. Relax your shoulders.
        You should be relaxed and alert. Tension is the enemy.

    c. Keep your hand relaxed.
        Your hand should be slightly cupped, as if you're holding a mouse.

2. Be an observer.
    Watch yourself. If you notice any tension, drop your shoulders again.

3. Work with a metronome.
    The metronome is your best friend. It will expose every deficiency so you can improve. Start as slow as you need to—usually at 60–80 beats per minute—in order to play each exercise smoothly and with no stumbling. Find the most difficult section of each exercise and slow down the tempo until you can play that section smoothly. Then, gradually increase the tempo. Set a goal of increasing the tempo 10 beats per minute, per week.

4. Play Smoothly.
    Slow, legato practice is the key to speed later on. The small muscles in your hands and forearms "remember" the motions involved in practicing, and if you play smoothly now, with no mistakes or stumbling, your playing will automatically get faster and more fluid.

5. Preparation, preparation, preparation.
    It's impossible to overstate the importance of preparation—it's the key to musicianship. Anticipate and visualize the next note to be played, and move the corresponding finger on your left hand over the appropriate fret *before* actually striking the note, while still holding the previous note.

Note: Track 1 contains tuning pitches.

ABOUT THE AUTHOR

Buzz Feiten started his professional career, while still in his teens, with an invitation to join the Paul Butterfield Blues Band. During his first night with the band, he jammed (on bass) in New York City with Butterfield, Al Kooper, B.B. King, and Jimi Hendrix. He was also with the Butterfield band when they played Woodstock. Buzz's natural gifts as a rhythm guitar player and as a passionate and melodic soloist have led him to record and perform with the likes of Stevie Wonder, Aretha Franklin, the Rascals, Gregg Allman, Bob Dylan, Rickie Lee Jones, Dave Sanborn, and Dave Weckl. He is also the inventor of the Buzz Feiten Tuning System.

The Buzz Feiten Model guitar is now available. To order Buzz's CDs, and for ordering information regarding the Buzz Feiten Model guitar, please visit www.buzzfeitenguitars.com, or email a request to buzz.feiten@yahoo.com.

Thanks for your support!

ACKNOWLEDGMENTS

I would like to give my deepest thanks to John Stix, Rebecca Skidmore, Susan Poliniak, and all the talented people who have supported me with encouragement and enthusiasm from the beginning.

CHAPTER 1

Warm-Ups

MAJOR SCALE

This one is designed to start the warm-up process. There are no big stretches involved—just "one finger per fret"—so it's a good way to get started. Remember, start slow and focus on preparing each finger to play the next note *before* leaving the previous note.

By the way, on the CD, every warm-up and exercise is played twice: once slowly, and then a second time at a faster tempo. Also, you may notice that I occasionally play slides, hammer-ons, and pull-offs—you should feel free to do likewise to suit the difficulty level that you want to achieve.

TRACK 02

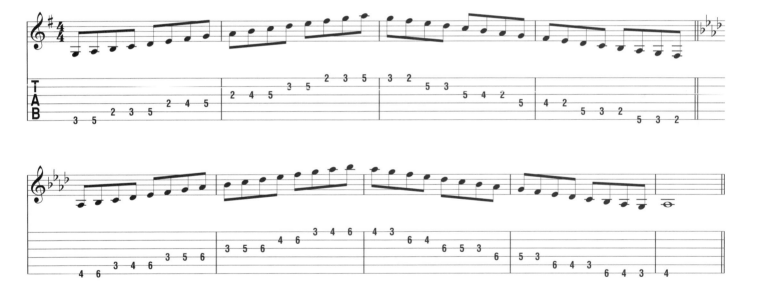

MAJOR SCALE STAIR-STEP 1

This one increases the difficulty slightly, including skips between strings and "stair steps." It improves the independence of the fingers on the left hand by increasing the distance each finger has to move in order to play the next note.

TRACK 03

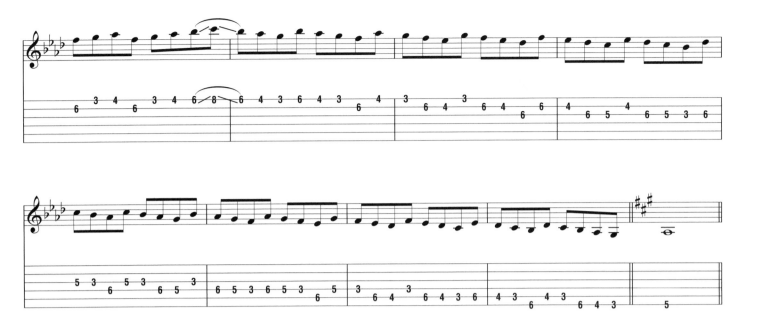

MAJOR SCALE STAIR-STEP 2

This warm-up is a variation on the stair-step movement in the previous one. It requires you to stretch your fingers in a slightly different way, and helps to increase your flexibility.

TRACK 04

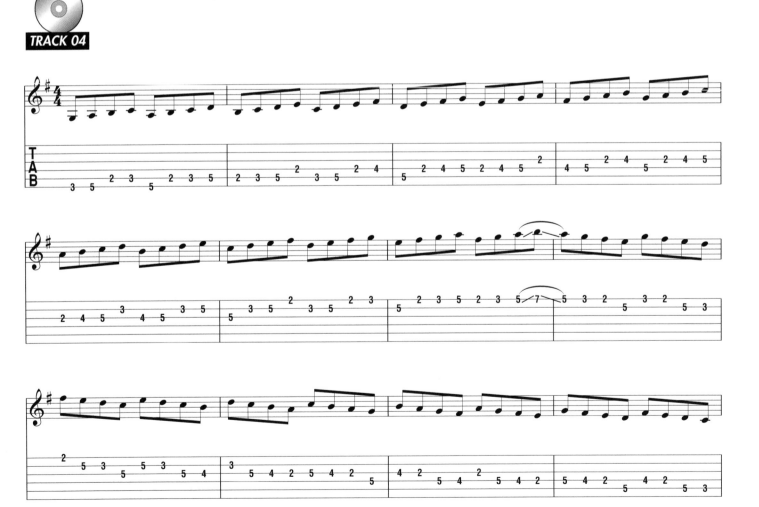

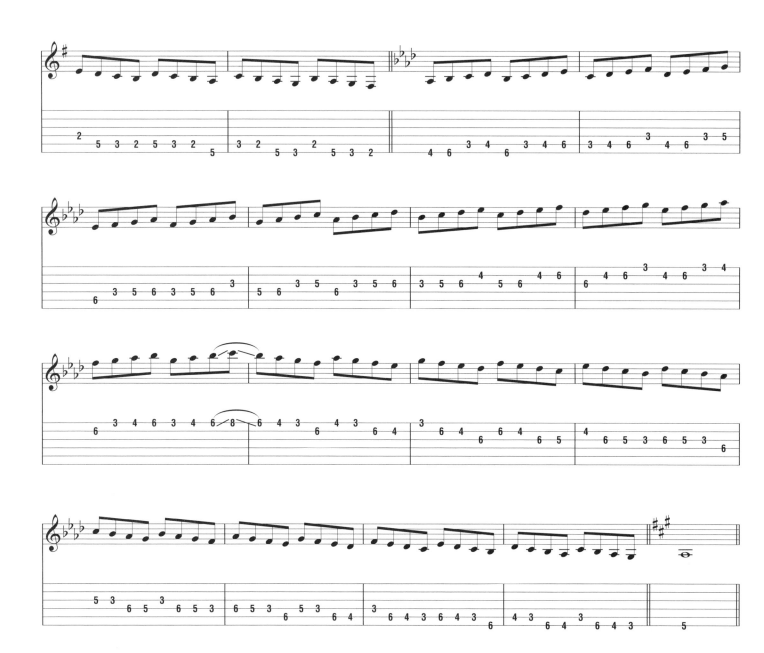

MAJOR ARPEGGIO

This warm-up is quite a bit more difficult than the previous ones because there are often big stretches between the fourth note of each four-note group and the first note of the following group. This one really works the fingers of your left hand. Remember to hold the fourth note of each group while preparing to play the first note of the next group. This warm-up also includes some position changes, adding difficulty to the left-hand finger stretches.

TRACK 05

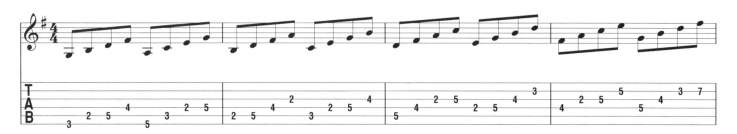

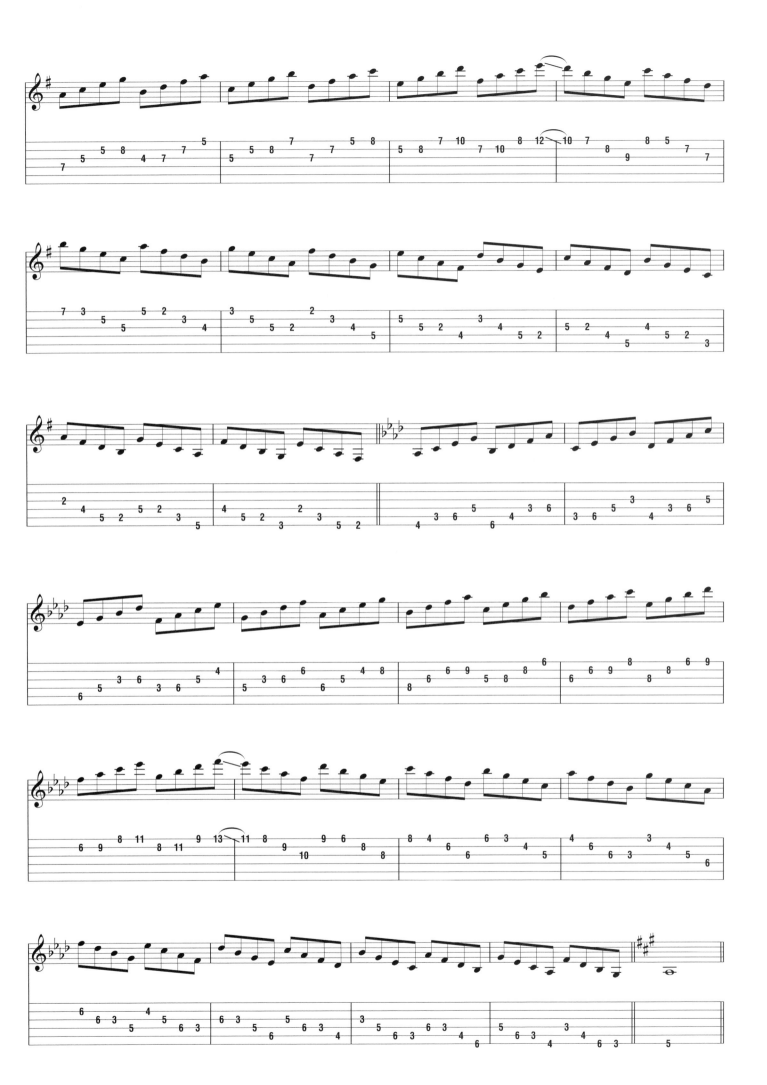

NATURAL MINOR SCALE

This warm-up is important because it makes you begin to think in a different key. The warm-ups and exercises in this book train your ears as well as your fingers because they are connected. The exercises in Chapters 2 and 3 focus on alternate harmonic structures, and this warm-up starts that process. It also improves finger independence because of the minor scale pattern.

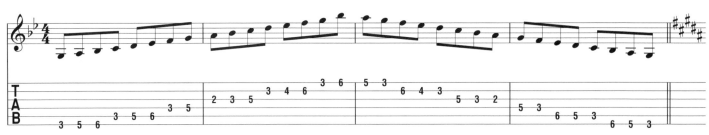

HARMONIC MINOR SCALE

This warm-up improves independence and is very good for your ear, because it is a different "shape" than the Natural Minor Scale warm-up. Harmonic minor scales can be very useful in Latin-based music because of the typical chord movement in that genre. A lot of fusion music uses Latin chord progressions.

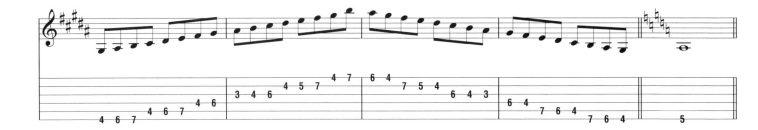

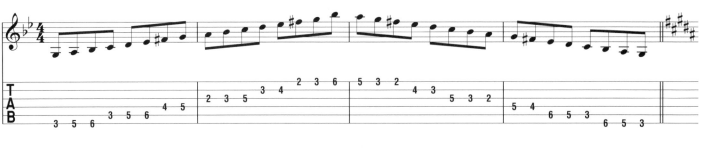

MINOR STAIR-STEP 1

As in the major stair-step warm-up, this one improves finger independence because of the string skips involved. However, this one adds a different harmonic element, which improves both your ears and your finger flexibility.

TRACK 08

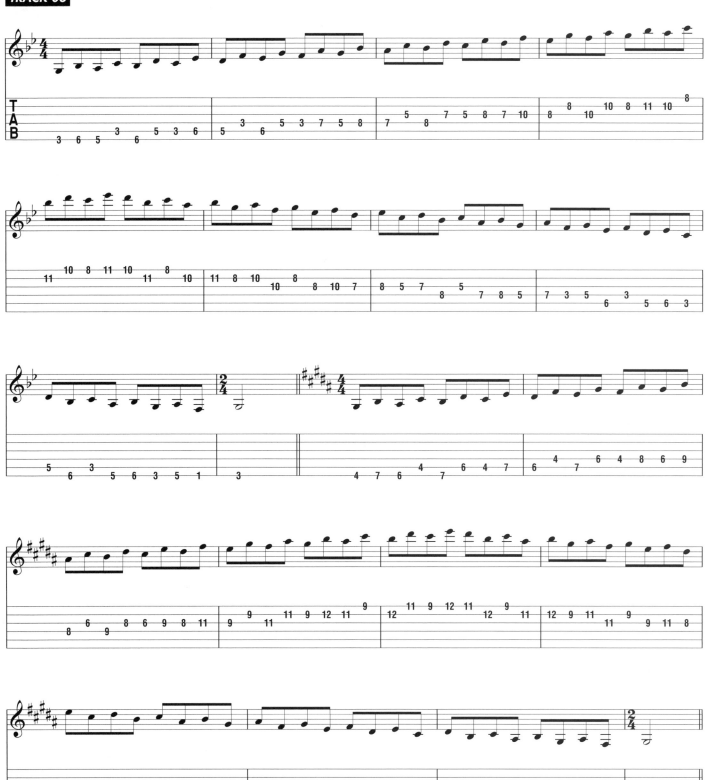

11

MINOR STAIR-STEP 2

This warm-up—which improves independence through some reversing of the stair-step direction—is a variation on the previous one.

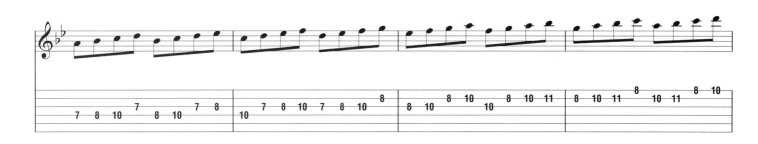

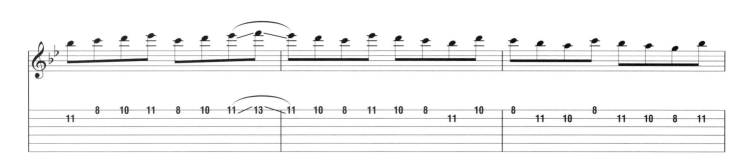

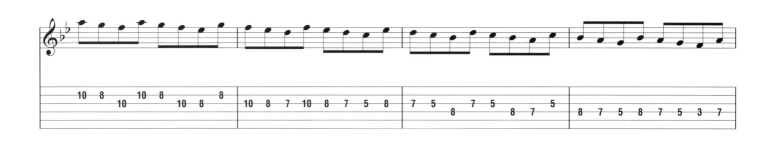

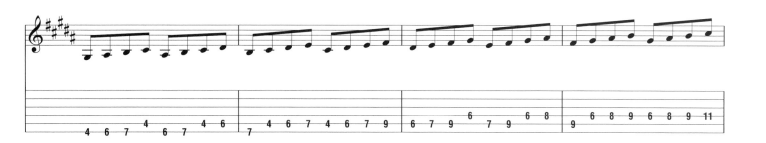

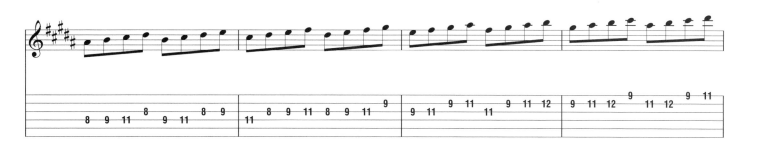

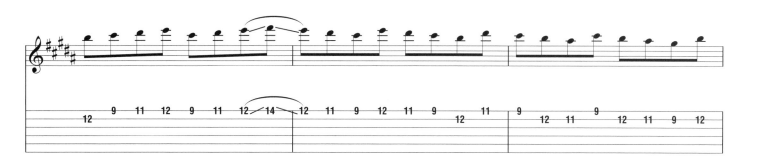

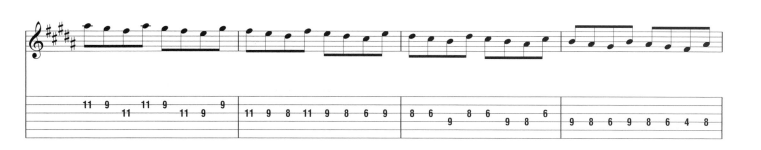

SOLOS

The following are examples of how the warm-ups in this chapter can be used as soloing ideas.

Buzz's Shuffle 1

TRACK 10   TRACK 11
Slow Demo
(First Two Choruses)

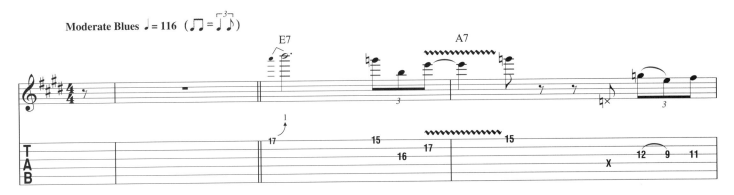

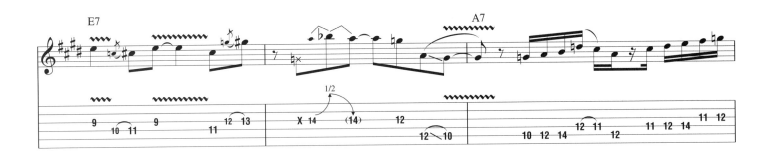

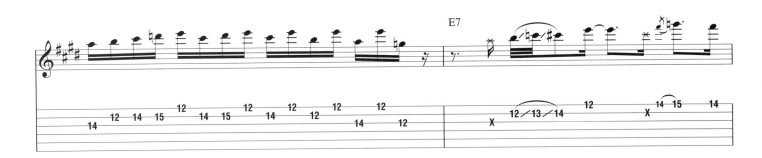

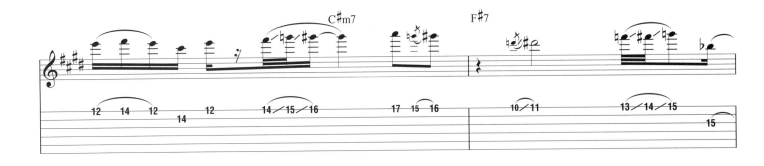

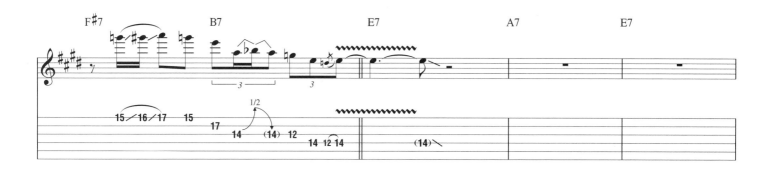

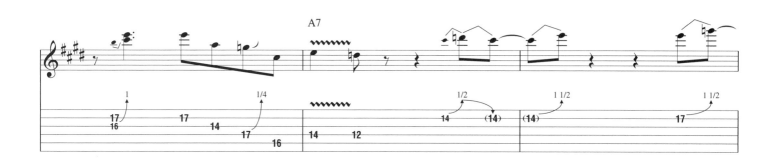

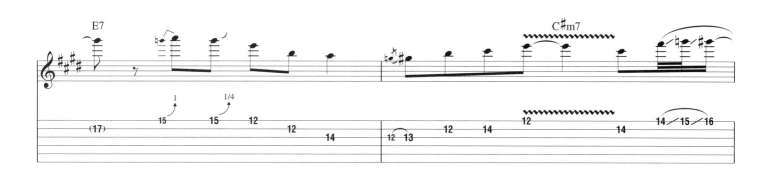

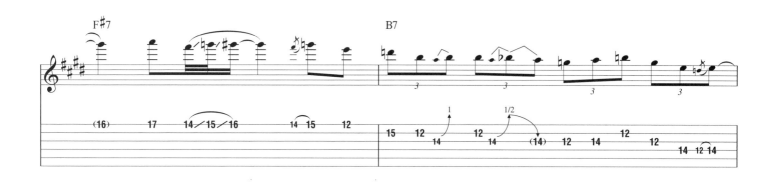

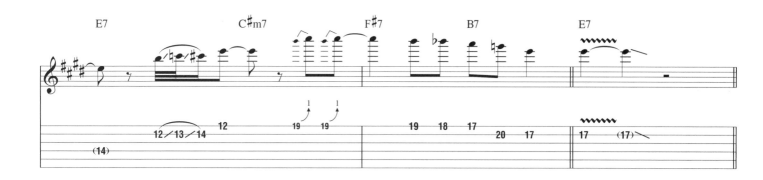

Buzz's Shuffle 2

Slow Demo

This track includes the backing for the above minus the solo guitar, so you can practice what you've learned in this chapter by playing through my solos and creating your own.

TRACK 14

CHAPTER 2
Intermediate Exercises

THIRDS

This exercise is designed to increase flexibility by introducing 3rds to a major scale pattern. The pattern skips to an adjacent string every few notes, and if you focus on preparing each finger for the next note to be played, your flexibility and finger independence will improve dramatically.

TRACK 15

SECOND-POSITION 3RDS

This exercise forces you to think in more than one position—this is very important in soloing. I had a major breakthrough when I realized that I could think in alternate positions on the neck. This exercise forces you out of that one-position thinking and adds harmonic interest and a wider range of notes to your solo ideas by moving further up the neck.

TRACK 16

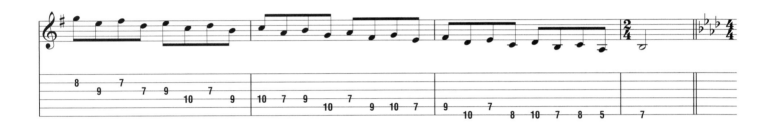

THIRD-POSITION 3RDS

This exercise is a variation on the previous one. It extends the number of notes available to you by moving even further up the neck.

 TRACK 17

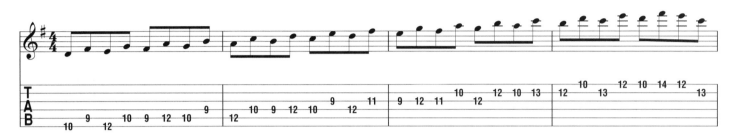

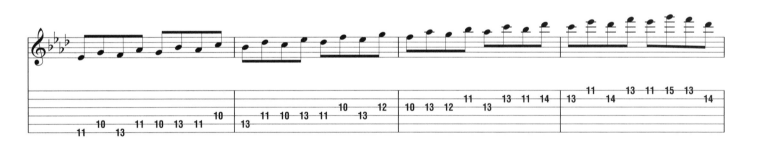

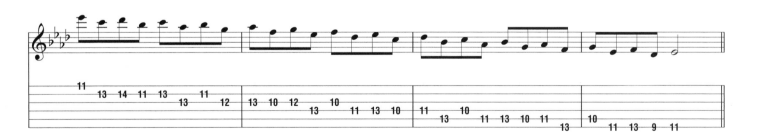

FOURTHS IN A MAJOR SCALE PATTERN

This exercise was another breakthrough for me. It combines major scale motion and 4ths, so there are a number of "double stops," in a way—meaning that you must play certain sequential notes by barring them with your pinky. This is a terrific exercise for pinky strength; it will dramatically improve your flexibility.

TRACK 18

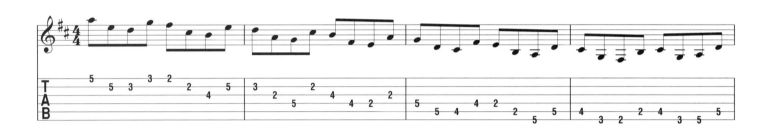

FOURTHS IN A MINOR SCALE PATTERN

This exercise is a variation on the previous one. It's the same pattern, but in a minor scale shape. The benefits are similar, but the minor harmonic element provides more options for solo ideas.

TRACK 19

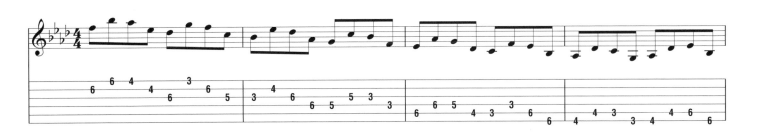

FIFTHS IN A SCALE PATTERN

This is one of the most important exercises in the book, because it combines major scale motion with a 5th interval skip every two notes. This exercise is terrific for both hand strength and overall flexibility. It also can be used very effectively in soloing because it has such interesting motion. This exercise can be played in both major and minor keys, depending on where you start the pattern. In a major key, you can start on the 2nd; for instance, in the key of C major you would start on D. In the key of C minor you would start the pattern on F, the 4th degree of the scale.

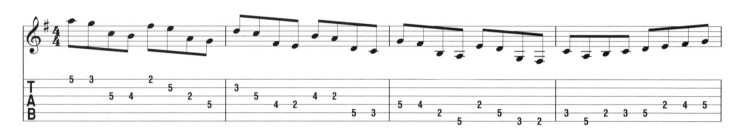

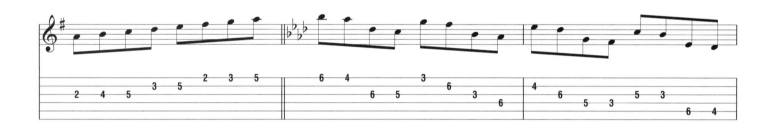

SIXTHS IN A MAJOR SCALE PATTERN

This exercise is very good for flexibility and independence because it includes such big interval skips. Once again, it is very important to prepare your finger for the next note to be played while holding the note you are playing as long as possible. This creates "muscle memory" in the fingers of your left hand, and your speed and accuracy are likely to improve if you focus on preparation. Pay attention to the slide between the 6th and 7th notes of the exercise.

TRACK 21

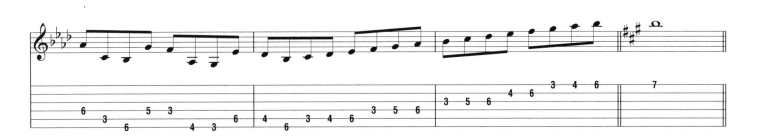

WHOLE TONE SCALE

This exercise is very effective in forcing you out of major/minor thinking only. Even though the whole tone mode is not commonly found in blues/rock, the more you can stretch yourself out of the one-finger-per-fret approach, the more you can start to see and hear other harmonic possibilities. The whole tone scale is very effective as a finger-stretching exercise because it consists of two-fret intervals. In a later exercise, you'll see how the whole tone diminished scale can be used in ii–V–I in blues/rock and fusion applications.

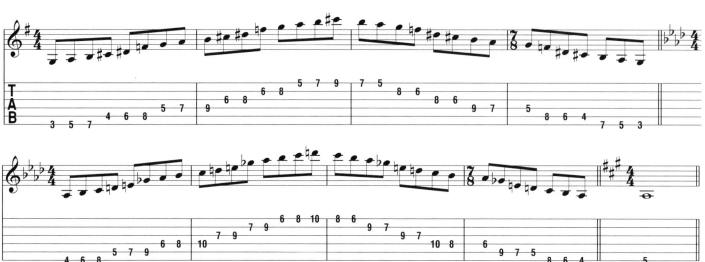

WHOLE TONE 3RDS IN A STAIR-STEP PATTERN

This exercise is a very effective finger-stretching tool; it also forces you into new harmonic shapes. The benefits of these alternate shapes will start to materialize over time as you become more proficient. These alternate modes and shapes will also start to appear in your playing as your ears and technique develop.

WHOLE TONE 3RDS IN AN UPWARD SCALE PATTERN

This exercise also stretches your ears into new harmonic territory.

TRACK 24

WHOLE TONE 3RDS IN A DOWNWARD SCALE PATTERN

This exercise is a variation on the previous one, and the benefits are similar.

SOLOS

The following are examples of how the exercises in this chapter can be used as soloing ideas.

Dinwiddie 1

Slow Demo

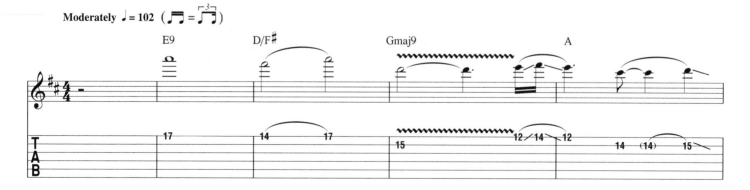

Dinwiddie 2

31

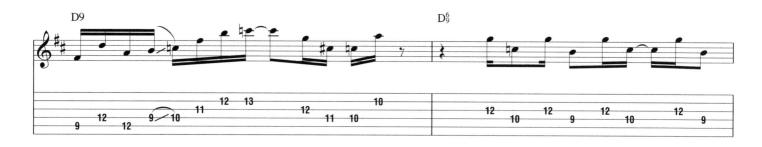

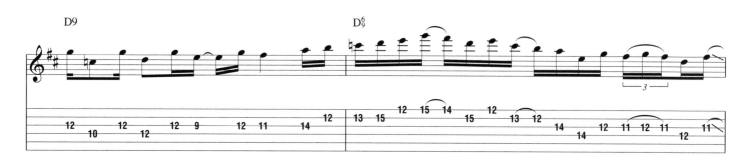

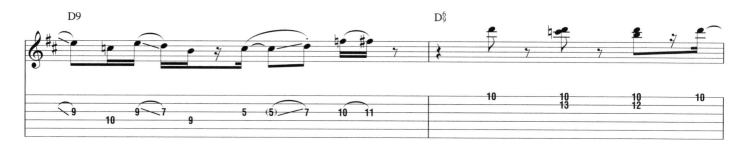

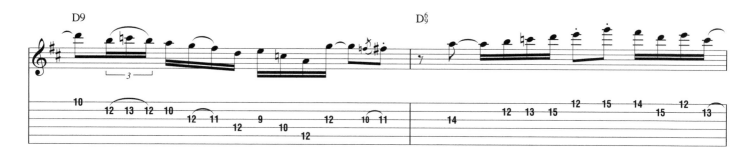

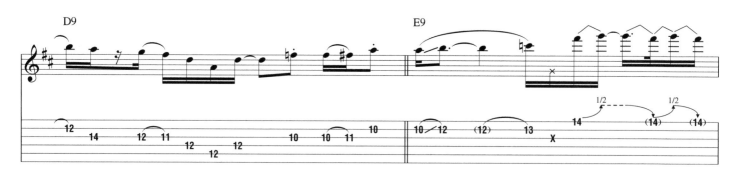

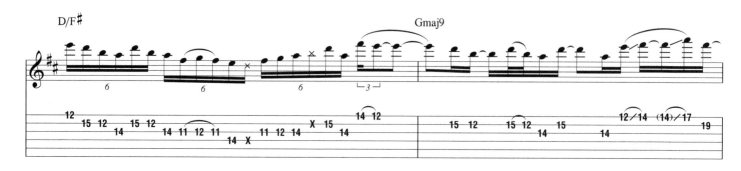

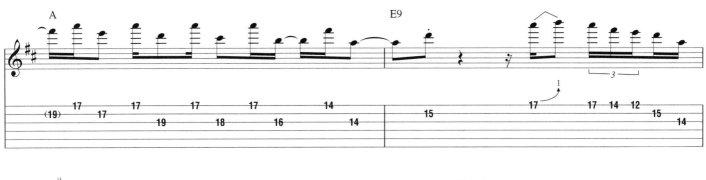

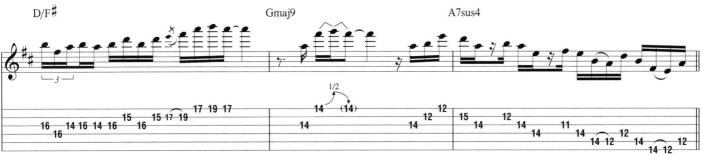

This track includes the backing for the above minus the solo guitar, so you can practice what you've learned in this chapter by playing through my solos and creating your own.

TRACK 30

CHAPTER 3

Advanced Exercises

DIMINISHED SCALE

This exercise is designed to push your ears in a new direction. I remember when I first became aware of diminished scales and their importance as "connecting" scales. They act as a bridge over ii–V–I chords. For instance, in an E minor blues, at the end of a chorus there is often a ii–V–I chord progression that looks like this:

F♯m7 (or F♯ diminished)   to   B7 (or B7♯5)   to   Em

This exercise helps to get you familiar with those shapes.

TRACK 31

DIMINISHED ARPEGGIO

This exercise is an extension of the previous exercise. It is terrific for stretching the fingers of your left hand; it also forces your ears in a new direction, and paves the way for the scale/arpeggio combinations you can use when soloing over ii–V–I. It is very important to concentrate on preparation here because of the big interval skips and the new sound of the diminished pattern.

DIMINISHED ARPEGGIO IN AN UPWARD PATTERN

This exercise is a variation on the previous one—it consists of four-note groups in a stair-step pattern. It is important to emphasize the first and fourth notes of each group, because that phrasing forces you to prepare each finger for the next note; it also tends to make the exercise sound smoother. The benefits are increased finger strength and flexibility, and improved ears.

TRACK 33

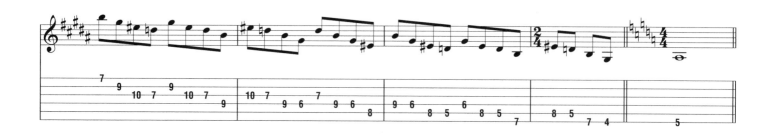

36

DIMINISHED ARPEGGIO IN A DOWNWARD PATTERN

This exercise is a variation on the previous one. The phrasing should be the same, but in the reverse direction. The benefits are similar, but the fingers are stretched in the opposite direction.

TRACK 34

DIMINISHED CHROMATIC 4THS

This exercise is fairly advanced, harmonically. It is also a very effective finger-strengthening tool because, like the Major Arpeggio warm-up in Chapter 1, it involves barring two notes with the pinky finger. This particular shape can sound great in a fusion solo over a V chord or an extension of a V chord.

TRACK 35

38

WHOLE TONE DIMINISHED SCALE

This exercise was another important breakthrough for me, and I remember David Sanborn teaching me this scale shortly after joining the Paul Butterfield Blues Band in 1968. I was very fortunate in that the guys in that band were very encouraging and supportive of me, teaching me different jazz songs, scales, etc., and exposing me to a whole new world of music.

This exercise is great for improving your ears. It also really forces you to prepare your fingers because of the unusual harmonic pattern and the combination of whole and half steps. This scale is very useful in fusion and jazz soloing over V7 chords.

WHOLE TONE DIMINISHED STAIR-STEP PATTERN

This exercise is a variation on the previous one, with an increased level of difficulty because of the addition of the stair-step pattern. The major benefits of this exercise are ear training and flexibility.

MINOR 9TH ARPEGGIO

This exercise on the top of the next page is based on arpeggios, and it's designed to really stretch your ears and left-hand fingers to the limit. There are big skips here, both physical and harmonic.

CHROMATIC 4THS

This exercise is primarily designed to stretch your ears and improve your right-hand string-to-string picking. It's fairly difficult to maintain this pattern all the way up and down the neck. Focus on playing the slides and picked notes as smoothly as possible.

TRACK 39

SOLOS

The following are examples of how the exercises in this chapter can be used as soloing ideas.

Jungle Walk 1

Slow Demo

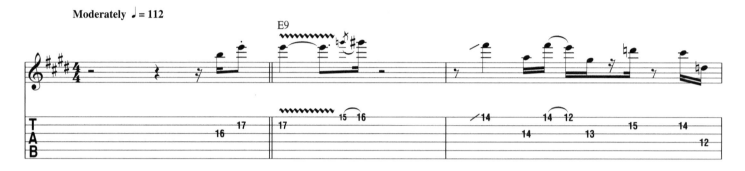

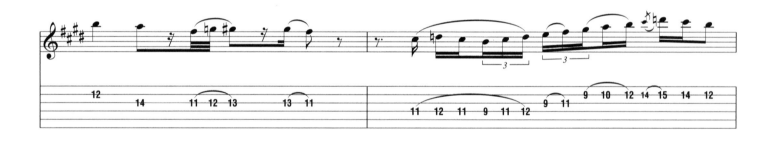

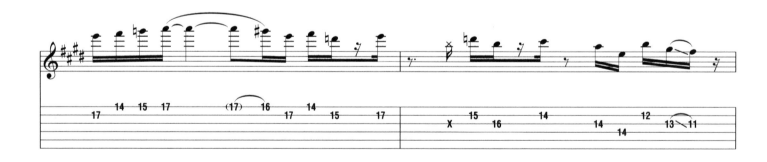

Jungle Walk 2

This track includes the backing for the above minus the solo guitar, so you can practice what you've learned in this chapter by playing through my solos and creating your own.

BUZZ FEITEN

A Selected Discography

BUZZ'S LATEST RELEASES

Buzz Feiten & The New Full Moon
Full Moon Live, Full Moon (the original studio recording re-released)
Buzz Feiten—*Whirlies*
Buzz Feiten & The Whirlies—*Live at The Baked Potato: Hollywood 6-4-99*

A SELECTION OF BUZZ'S OTHER RECORDINGS

Gregg Allman—*Laid Back*
George Benson—*George Benson Collection*
Stephen Bishop—*Red Cab to Manhattan*
The Paul Butterfield Blues Band—*Keep on Moving*
Felix Cavaliere—*Destiny*
Chicago—*Chicago 18*
Gene Clark—*No Other*
Commander Cody & The Lost…—*Flying Dreams*
Randy Crawford—*Windsong*
Bob Dylan—*New Morning*
Aretha Franklin—*Spirit in the Dark; One Lord, One Faith, One Baptism*
Michael Franks—*Blue Pacific*
Footlose—*Original Soundtrack*
Free Creek—*Summit Meeting*
Full Moon—*Full Moon*
Stefan Grossman—*Perspective*
Hall & Oates—*Change of Season*
Stuart Hamm—*Kings of Sleep, Urge*
Fareed Haque—*Sacred Addicition*
Rickie Lee Jones—*Rickie Lee Jones, Pirates, Flying Cowboys*
Bobby King & Terry Evans—*Rhythm, Blues Soul & Grooves*
Dave Koz—*Dave Koz, Lucky Man*
Labelle—*Pressure Cookin'*
Neil Larsen—*Jungle Fever, High Gear*
Larsen-Feiten Band—*Larsen-Feiten Band, Full Moon*
Kenny Loggins—*Vox Humana*
Jeff Lorber—*Private Passion, Worth Waiting For*
Love—*Reel to Real*
Don McLean—*Don McLean*
Larry John McNally—*Fade to Black*

Bette Midler—*Experience the Divine*
Randy Newman—*Land of Dreams*
The Young Rascals—*Peaceful World, Island of Real*
David Sanborn—*Taking Off, Voyeur*
Boz Scaggs—*Other Roads*
Tom Scott—*Street Beat*
Ben Sidran—*Cat and the Hat*
Edwin Starr—*Stronger Than You Think I Am*
Syreeta—*Syreeta*
Livingston Taylor—*Over the Rainbow*
Jennifer Warnes—*Shot Through the Heart*
Dave Wecki—*Rhythm of the Soul, Synergy*
Stevie Wonder—*Music of My Mind, Talking Book, Songs in the Key of Life*

Great DVD selections from CHERRY LANE

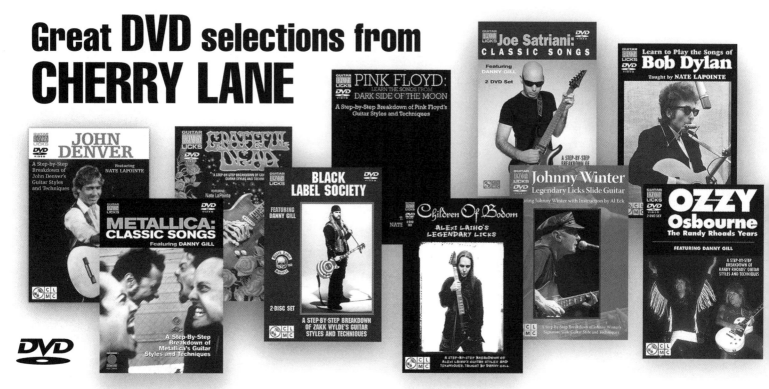

Steven Adler's Getting Started with Rock Drumming
taught by the Legendary Former Guns N' Roses Drummer!
02501387 DVD $29.99

Altered Tunings and Techniques for Modern Metal Guitar
taught by Rick Plunkett
02501457 DVD $19.99

Beginning Blues Guitar
RHYTHM AND SOLOS
taught by Al Ek
02501325 DVD $19.99

Black Label Society
featuring Danny Gill
Guitar Legendary Licks
02500983 2-DVD Set $29.95

Black Sabbath
featuring Danny Gill
Guitar Legendary Licks
02500874 DVD $24.95

Blues Masters by the Bar
taught by Dave Celentano
02501146 DVD $24.99

Children of Bodom
ALEXI LAIHO'S LEGENDARY LICKS
taught by Danny Gill
02501398 DVD $24.99

Classical Guitar Favorites
featuring Danny Gill
Guitar Legendary Licks
02500899 DVD $24.95

John Denver
featuring Nate LaPointe
Guitar Legendary Licks
02500917 DVD $24.95

Learn to Play the Songs of Bob Dylan
taught by Nate LaPointe
Guitar Legendary Licks
02500918 DVD $24.95

Funky Rhythm Guitar
taught by Buzz Feiten
02501393 DVD $24.99

Grateful Dead – Classic Songs
featuring Nate LaPointe
Guitar Legendary Licks
02500968 DVD $24.95

Grateful Dead
featuring Nate LaPointe
Guitar Legendary Licks
02500551 DVD $24.95

Guitar Heroes
taught by Danny Gill
Guitar Legendary Licks
02501069 2-DVD Set $29.95

Home Recording Presents: Miking Guitars in the Studio
featuring Steven Lee
02500629 DVD $24.95

The Latin Funk Connection
02501417 DVD $19.99

Life of the Party
PLAY PIANO IN AN INSTANT
by Bill Gulino
Hosted by John Sebastian
02500725 Book/CD/DVD Pack $49.95

Metallica – 1983-1988
featuring Doug Boduch
Bass Legendary Licks
02500481 DVD $24.95

Metallica – 1988-1997
featuring Doug Boduch
Bass Legendary Licks
02500484 DVD $24.95

Metallica – 1983-1988
featuring Nathan Kilen
Drum Legendary Licks
02500482 DVD $24.95

Metallica – 1988-1997
featuring Nathan Kilen
Drum Legendary Licks
02500485 DVD $24.95

Metallica – 1983-1988
featuring Doug Boduch
Guitar Legendary Licks
02500479 DVD $24.95

Metallica – 1988-1997
featuring Doug Boduch
Guitar Legendary Licks
02500480 DVD $24.99

Metallica: Classic Songs
featuring Danny Gill
Bass Legendary Licks
02500841 DVD $24.95

Metallica: Classic Songs
featuring Jack E. Roth
Drum Legendary Licks
02500839 DVD $24.95

Metallica: Classic Songs
featuring Danny Gill
Guitar Legendary Licks
02500840 DVD $24.95

Mastering the Modes for the Rock Guitarist
taught by Dave Celentano
02501449 DVD $19.99

Home Recording Magazine's 100 Recording Tips and Tricks
STRATEGIES AND SOLUTIONS FOR YOUR HOME STUDIO
02500509 DVD $19.95

Ozzy Osbourne – The Randy Rhoads Years
featuring Danny Gill
Guitar Legendary Licks
02501301 2-DVD Set $29.99

Pink Floyd – Learn the Songs from Dark Side of the Moon
by Nate LaPointe
Guitar Legendary Licks
02500919 DVD $24.95

Poncho Sanchez
featuring the Poncho Sanchez Latin Jazz Band
02500729 DVD $24.95

Joe Satriani
featuring Danny Gill
Guitar Legendary Licks Series
02500767 2-DVD Set $29.95

Joe Satriani – Classic Songs
featuring Danny Gill
Guitar Legendary Licks
02500913 2-DVD Set $29.95

The Latin Funk Connection
02501417 DVD $24.99

Johnny Winter
taught by Al Ek
Guitar Legendary Licks
02501307 2-DVD Set 29.99

Johnny Winter
SLIDE GUITAR
featuring Johnny Winter with instruction by Al Ek
Guitar Legendary Licks
02501042 DVD $29.95

Wolfmother
featuring Danny Gill
02501062 DVD $24.95

See your local music retailer or contact

EXCLUSIVELY DISTRIBUTED BY
HAL•LEONARD CORPORATION
7777 W. BLUEMOUND RD. P.O. BOX 13819 MILWAUKEE, WI 53213

Prices, contents, and availability subject to change without notice.

08